MW01702936

Book E

Specific Skill Series
for Language Arts

Spelling

Leveled Books
in Nine Key
Language Arts Skill Areas

SRA
Columbus, OH

The McGraw·Hill Companies

Cover: ©PhotoDisc/Getty Images, Inc.

SRAonline.com

SRA

Send all inquiries to:
SRA/McGraw-Hill
8787 Orion Place
Columbus, OH 43240-4027

Printed in the United States of America.

ISBN 0-07-601704-4

3 4 5 6 7 8 9 RHR 15 14 13 12 11 10

TO THE TEACHER

GENERAL INFORMATION ON SPELLING

The most recent studies in spelling development have shown that students do not learn to spell by memorizing word lists, as in the past. Rather, students become competent spellers by learning spelling concepts, patterns, rules, and exceptions to those rules. The chart below lists strategies that can help students learn to spell. With practice, students can learn when it is appropriate to employ the different strategies to help them spell most English words.

Sound Pattern Strategies	Structural Pattern Strategies	Meaning Pattern Strategies
Pronunciation Visualization Consonant Substitution Vowel Substitution	Conventions Strategy	Family Strategy Meaning Strategy Compound Word Strategy Foreign Language Strategy Proofreading Strategy Dictionary Strategy

ABOUT ***SPECIFIC SKILL SERIES FOR LANGUAGE ARTS***

Specific Skill Series for Language Arts is a companion to ***Specific Skill Series,*** a supplemental reading program that has been widely recognized for its effectiveness for over thirty years. The two series are designed and organized the same. ***Specific Skill Series for Language Arts*** consists of discrete units of practice exercises that target and reinforce fundamental language-arts skills. Units in both series are presented in multiple-choice format for standardized test practice.

ABOUT ***SPELLING***

The scope and sequence for Books A through H of *Spelling* focuses on spelling strategies rather than memorization of word lists. The scope and sequence for each book is located on the last page of the book. Each unit includes

- **rule boxes** that explain spelling strategies.
- **models** in each rule box to illustrate the strategies.
- **multiple-choice exercises** for skills practice and reinforcement.

Four **Language Activity Pages** (LAPs) appear in each book. Each LAP is divided into the following four sections and reviews the skills practiced in the preceding units:

Exercising Your Skill reviews key terms and concepts.

Expanding Your Skill provides mixed practice.

Exploring Language shows how the skills apply to real-world contexts by featuring one of six forms of writing: descriptive, narrative, personal, persuasive, expository, and poetry.

Expressing Yourself includes two creative activities related to the skills. One activity is always a Work-with-a-Partner activity to encourage collaborative learning.

TO THE TEACHER

SERIES COMPONENTS

- **Student Editions:** Nine books in each level (A–H) focus on nine skill areas: *Grammar, Usage, Mechanics, Spelling, Vocabulary, Sentences, Paragraphs, Writing Process,* and *Research.*
- **Placement Test Books:** One book for each skill area includes diagnostic tests to place students in the correct level.
- **Teacher's Manual:** Primarily an answer key, the *Teacher's Manual* also includes reproducible student worksheets and further information on how to use the program, including classroom management tips.

HOW TO USE *SPECIFIC SKILL SERIES FOR LANGUAGE ARTS*

Placing Students in Levels: The scope and sequence, complexity of skills, and readability in Levels A through H correspond to Grades 1 through 8. Students may, however, be placed in any level. For example, in the second grade, a student who needs remedial work in a specific skill may be placed in Book A, an on-level student who would benefit from skills reinforcement may be placed in Book B, and an advanced student who is ready for enrichment may be placed in Book C or higher. *Placement Tests* help place students in the correct level.

Setting: This series can be used for independent study and one-on-one practice sessions, as well as in small-group and whole-class settings. It is also effective in after-school and summer-school programs.

Getting Started: Students must have notebook paper or copies of reproducible student worksheets (located in the *Teacher's Manual*) before they begin working. Remind students not to write in the books. Students may begin in any unit of any book, depending on the skill practice they need, although it is recommended that they begin with Unit 1. As they work through the units, students should record their answers on notebook paper or on the student worksheets.

Pacing: Students should be encouraged to work at their own pace, completing a few units every day or every other day.

Scoring: Teachers should score units as soon as they have been completed. Then a discussion can be held in which students justify their answer choices.

Internet Use: Some activities, especially those in *Research,* require students to use the Internet. Students' use of the Internet should be monitored closely for content appropriateness and safety.

TO THE STUDENT

It is always important to spell words correctly when you write. It is possible to become a better speller by learning and applying spelling strategies.

In Book E *Spelling,* you will learn about spelling words

- by identifying spelling patterns in words that rhyme.
- by following rules for adding endings.
- by thinking about the way they look.
- by thinking about how they are combined to form compound words.
- by thinking about what they mean.
- by referring to the dictionary.
- by proofreading your work to check for spelling errors.
- by thinking about base words and other words in the same word family.
- by understanding root words from other languages.

After you complete this book, you will know that many sounds can be spelled more than one way. Spelling variations for the /əl/ sound are boldfaced below.

The cat wore a comic**al** expression.

Your penc**il** is under Ted's chair.

Vermont is America's largest producer of map**le** syrup.

You will also learn that many words and spelling patterns in the English language are based on foreign languages, such as French, Italian, and German.

In French, the /ā/ sound is often spelled *e*.

In German, the /ou/ sound is often spelled *au*.

At Mario's caf**é**, you can order s**au**erkr**au**t with a side of macaron**i**.

Many Italian words end with a vowel.

As you master the skills in this book, you will be able to avoid common spelling errors in your work by using the spelling strategies you have learned.

Unit 1

Rhyming Strategy

Rhyming words have the same ending vowel and consonant sounds.

- Rhyming words sometimes have the same spelling pattern.

  br**ight**, m**ight**

  t**oast**, r**oast**

- Sometimes rhyming words have different spelling patterns.

  rise, **prize**

  cone, **sewn**

Animal Facts

Choose the word that rhymes with each underlined word. Notice that rhyming words may have different spelling patterns.

1. The <u>stripes</u> on a zebra help it to hide from predators.
   (A) drips **(B)** wipes **(C)** strikes **(D)** lines

2. An elephant can stay cool by splashing water over its <u>head</u> with its trunk.
   (A) spread **(B)** bead **(C)** greed **(D)** pleasant

3. A baby kangaroo finishes growing inside the pouch of its <u>mother</u>.
   (A) bother **(B)** father **(C)** another **(D)** together

4. The <u>wings</u> of a hummingbird can flap up to seventy times per second.
   (A) find **(B)** tin **(C)** wind **(D)** strings

5. Bees collect nectar from flowers to make <u>honey</u>.
   (A) funny **(B)** phone **(C)** home **(D)** hunter

6. Beavers can cut down trees with their <u>front</u> teeth.
   (A) font **(B)** punt **(C)** mount **(D)** note

7. A flamingo's beak works like a <u>sieve</u> to strain food.
   (A) sleeve **(B)** fleece **(C)** vein **(D)** give

8. Gazelles <u>lope</u> across the plains and deserts of Africa.
   (A) swoop **(B)** flop **(C)** soap **(D)** moat

9. The song of the chickadee <u>imitates</u> its name.
   (A) acrobats **(B)** bakes **(C)** infants **(D)** penetrates

Word Meanings

10. The word *seize* means to take hold of something suddenly.
(A) knees (B) receive (C) agreed (D) piece

11. The word *reign* means to have royal power.
(A) seen (B) strain (C) piece (D) find

12. The word *height* means how tall something is.
(A) eight (B) great (C) knight (D) freight

13. The word *known* means that you already knew something.
(A) blow (B) bow (C) coach (D) stone

14. The word *amuse* means to make someone laugh.
(A) choose (B) house (C) due (D) us

15. The word *peace* means freedom from war.
(A) least (B) breeze (C) greed (D) niece

16. The word *retrieve* means to get something back.
(A) relief (B) receive (C) deceit (D) alleviate

17. The word *shrewd* means clever or keen.
(A) flowed (B) broom (C) rude (D) few

18. The word *droop* means to sag or to wilt.
(A) soup (B) balloon (C) prop (D) youth

19. The word *burrow* means to dig.
(A) route (B) thorough (C) through (D) eyebrow

20. The word *sustain* means to support.
(A) diagram (B) charm (C) airplane (D) armchair

Unit 1
Rhyming Strategy

Choose the word that does *not* rhyme with each underlined word. Notice that rhyming words may have different spelling patterns.

21. Hurricane Andrew <u>destroyed</u> many houses.
(A) employed **(B)** annoyed **(C)** void **(D)** loyal

22. The president of the United States can <u>appoint</u> people to special jobs.
(A) anoint **(B)** point **(C)** font **(D)** joint

23. A <u>room</u> usually has four walls.
(A) gloom **(B)** perfume **(C)** tomb **(D)** comb

24. Hungry lions <u>devour</u> their prey.
(A) pour **(B)** hour **(C)** tower **(D)** sour

25. <u>Chowder</u> is usually made with clams and potatoes.
(A) powder **(B)** founder **(C)** louder **(D)** prouder

26. Many houses are made of <u>wood</u>.
(A) should **(B)** mood **(C)** could **(D)** stood

27. Tomatoes and peppers are <u>fruits</u>.
(A) boots **(B)** flutes **(C)** fluids **(D)** shoots

28. High hedges around curved paths form <u>mazes</u> in gardens.
(A) raises **(B)** races **(C)** phrases **(D)** praises

29. Tree <u>ferns</u> can grow to be fifty feet tall.
(A) turns **(B)** earns **(C)** returns **(D)** farms

30. Blackbeard the pirate shared his <u>plunder</u> with others.
(A) hunger **(B)** under **(C)** wonder **(D)** thunder

31. Abraham Lincoln did not want to <u>deny</u> freedom to any person.
(A) eye **(B)** sigh **(C)** beside **(D)** lie

Unit 1
Rhyming Strategy

Remember that vowel sounds can have a variety of spellings. Look at these rhyming words, and notice the different vowel spellings for the same sound.

- The /o͞o/ sound can be spelled *ew* as in *kn<u>ew</u>* and *oo* as in *z<u>oo</u>.*
- The /ô/ sound can be spelled *au* as in *h<u>au</u>l* and *aw* as in *cr<u>aw</u>l.*

The Human Body

Choose the word that does *not* rhyme with each underlined word. Notice that rhyming words may have different spelling patterns.

32. People have four kinds of teeth to <u>chew</u> food.
(A) knew **(B)** glue **(C)** do **(D)** go

33. The human <u>tongue</u> can taste foods that are sweet, salty, sour, and bitter.
(A) among **(B)** lung **(C)** sung **(D)** fun

34. The stomach is one of the organs that digests <u>food</u>.
(A) mood **(B)** good **(C)** rude **(D)** sued

35. People <u>yawn</u> when they need to get more oxygen.
(A) lawn **(B)** gone **(C)** lone **(D)** pawn

36. Teardrops are mostly made of <u>salt</u>.
(A) fault **(B)** vault **(C)** dealt **(D)** malt

37. Tears flow <u>through</u> ducts that open to the inner corner of the eye.
(A) rough **(B)** grew **(C)** slew **(D)** hue

38. A person uses about forty-three muscles to <u>frown</u>.
(A) noun **(B)** flown **(C)** clown **(D)** town

39. Scientists continue to <u>pursue</u> cures for diseases.
(A) crew **(B)** issue **(C)** canoe **(D)** foot

40. Regular exercise may <u>stall</u> the effects of aging on the human body.
(A) lull **(B)** fall **(C)** bawl **(D)** overhaul

Unit 2

Conventions Strategy

Adding endings can cause some base-word spelling changes.

- For most words, simply add *-er, -est, -ed, -ing,* or *-s.*

    sweet → sweet**er**, sweet**est**

    complain → complain**ed**, complain**ing**, complain**s**

- When necessary, double the final consonant, or change *y* to *i* before adding an ending.

    admit → admit**ted**, admit**ting**

    drowsy → drows**ier**, drows**iest**

- When a base word ends in *ch, sh, s, ss, x, z,* or *zz,* add *-es* to write most plural forms.

    church**es**, wish**es**, bus**es**, class**es**, tax**es**, waltz**es**, quiz**zes**

The Rhino

Choose the correct form of the underlined word to complete each sentence.

1. A rhinoceros has a long <u>curve</u> horn sticking up from its nose.
   (A) curving **(B)** curveing **(C)** curvying **(D)** curvving

2. The rhinoceros is one of the <u>husky</u> animals because of its large solid body and short legs.
   (A) huskyest **(B)** huskkest **(C)** huskiest **(D)** huskkiest

3. The rhinoceros is <u>relate</u> to the horse.
   (A) relatted **(B)** related **(C)** relatied **(D)** relatyed

4. Rhinoceroses can be seen, or <u>spot</u>, in Africa and Asia.
   (A) spoted **(B)** spotied **(C)** spotyed **(D)** spotted

5. However, much of this animal's habitat has been <u>destroy</u>.
   (A) destroyed **(B)** destroied **(C)** destroyyed **(D)** destroed

6. Rhinoceroses may live on open grasslands or in <u>marsh</u>.
   (A) marshes **(B)** marshs **(C)** marshies **(D)** marshys

7. A rhinoceros <u>possess</u> a keen sense of hearing and of smell.
   (A) possessis **(B)** possessez **(C)** possesses **(D)** possess

Unit 2

Conventions Strategy

A Bestseller

8. There are a lot of steps to take when publish a book.
(A) publishing (B) publishhing (C) publisheing (D) publishying

9. Before a manuscript is submit, an author usually hires an agent.
(A) submited (B) submitted (C) submitied (D) submityed

10. The agent is usually the one who negotiate the financial deal.
(A) negotiaties (B) negotiats (C) negotiattes (D) negotiates

11. The publisher and the agent agree on how much of the royalty the author will receive.
(A) royaltys (B) royaltes (C) royalties (D) royaltties

12. Editors are permit to make changes to the author's manuscript.
(A) permitted (B) permited (C) permyted (D) permittied

13. Printing of the book can be delay if many changes are made.
(A) delayyed (B) delayed (C) dellayed (D) delaied

14. Most authors hope their book will sell out the quick.
(A) quickiest (B) quickkest (C) quickest (D) quickyest

15. A bookstore often attach a price sticker to a book's cover.
(A) attaches (B) attachs (C) attachies (D) attachyes

16. Promote a book takes effort by both the author and the publisher.
(A) Promoteing (B) Promoteng (C) Promotieng (D) Promoting

17. Nonfiction books like biography often become bestsellers.
(A) biographys (B) biographies (C) biographyes (D) biographis

Unit 2
Conventions Strategy

Choose the word that should have the final consonant doubled before adding the given ending.

18. *-ed*
(A) stop (B) dream (C) fail (D) hope

19. *-ing*
(A) portray (B) match (C) prefer (D) fix

20. *-er*
(A) light (B) split (C) enable (D) happy

21. *-est*
(A) faint (B) fast (C) foggy (D) fit

22. *-ed*
(A) land (B) commit (C) spy (D) delay

23. *-ing*
(A) refer (B) teach (C) repeat (D) post

24. *-est*
(A) silly (B) cute (C) loud (D) hot

25. *-er*
(A) steep (B) new (C) flat (D) grand

26. *-ed*
(A) hurry (B) plan (C) accept (D) agree

27. *-ing*
(A) snarl (B) wail (C) lurk (D) cram

28. *-est*
(A) slim (B) sweet (C) swift (D) fast

29. *-ed*
(A) award (B) prop (C) flatter (D) focus

Unit 2
Conventions Strategy

Choose the word that has correctly added the given ending.

30. *-s* or *-es*
(A) ally → allies
(B) pulley → pullies
(C) march → marchs
(D) delay → delayes

31. *-d* or *-ed*
(A) worry → worryed
(B) deploy → deployyed
(C) commit → committed
(D) prey → preyied

32. *-d* or *-ed*
(A) journey → journeyyed
(B) apply → applied
(C) convey → conveyied
(D) fault → faultied

33. *-er*
(A) gray → grayier
(B) early → earlyer
(C) sandy → sandyer
(D) fuzzy → fuzzier

34. *-s* or *-es*
(A) deputy → deputys
(B) survey → surveys
(C) holiday → holidayes
(D) valley → valleyies

35. *-est*
(A) salty → saltiest
(B) cozy → cozyest
(C) crazy → crazyiest
(D) wealthy → wealthyest

36. *-s* or *-es*
(A) display → displayes
(B) relay → relaies
(C) gash → gashs
(D) convoy → convoys

37. *-er*
(A) cold → coldder
(B) warm → warmmer
(C) hot → hoter
(D) chilly → chillier

38. *-d* or *-ed*
(A) employ → employyed
(B) petrify → petrified
(C) annoy → annoied
(D) spray → sprayied

Unit 2

Conventions Strategy

Some plurals are irregular.

- The spelling of the base word changes to form the plural.

mouse ⟶ m**ice** calf ⟶ cal**ves**

- Some plural forms are the same as their singular forms.

One **moose** was in the woods. Ten **moose** were in the woods.

In the Kitchen

Choose the correct plural form of the underlined word to complete each sentence.

39. It takes about six cups of flour to make two loaf of bread.
    (A) loafs **(B)** loafes **(C)** loaves **(D)** loaffs

40. The average American eats about fifteen dozen eggs each year.
    (A) dozenes **(B)** dozen **(C)** dozens **(D)** dozenns

41. Eating too many cakes and cookies is bad for your tooth.
    (A) tooths **(B)** tooth **(C)** toothes **(D)** teeth

42. Different knife are used for cutting bread, meat, and vegetables.
    (A) knives **(B)** knifes **(C)** kniffes **(D)** knife

43. Julia Child is one of the most famous woman in the world of cooking.
    (A) womans **(B)** womanes **(C)** women **(D)** womens

44. The leaf of mint and parsley add flavor to many dishes.
    (A) leafes **(B)** leafs **(C)** leaffes **(D)** leaves

45. The meat of deer may be roasted in the oven.
    (A) deers **(B)** deer **(C)** deeres **(D)** deeries

46. Goose are often roasted instead of turkeys for holiday meals.
    (A) Gooses **(B)** Geeses **(C)** Geese **(D)** Goose

47. Grapefruit half can be sweetened with sugar.
    (A) halves **(B)** halfs **(C)** halfes **(D)** halvies

Unit 2
Conventions Strategy

Words that end in *o* form plurals in different ways.

- For words that end in a consonant and *o*, the plural is usually formed by adding *-es*.

  tomato ⟶ tomato**es**

- For words that end in a vowel and *o*, the plural is usually formed by adding *-s*.

  radio ⟶ radio**s**

Sometimes there is more than one correct, or accepted, way to form the plural of a word, especially words that end in *o*.

buffalo ⟶ buffalo *or* buffalo**es**

Use a dictionary to check the plural spelling of a word if you are unsure.

Choose the correct plural form of the underlined word to complete each sentence.

48. A cave produces great echo when you yell.
(A) echo (B) echoes (C) echoos

49. Patio are usually paved with bricks or flat stones.
(A) Patios (B) Patioes (C) Patio

50. Musicians record their music in recording studio.
(A) studio (B) studios (C) studioes

51. Heracles is one of the great hero of ancient Greece.
(A) heroses (B) heroes (C) hero

52. Most popular rock bands make video that go with their songs.
(A) videoes (B) video (C) videos

53. President Franklin Roosevelt used over 600 veto while in office.
(A) vetos (B) vetoos (C) vetoes

54. One billion is the number one followed by nine zero.
(A) zerois (B) zero (C) zeros

The First LAP
Language Activity Pages

A. Exercising Your Skill

You have been learning about using the rhyming strategy and the conventions strategy to spell words. Number your paper from 1 to 8. Answer the following questions by writing **T** for true or **F** for false.

1. Each vowel sound has only one spelling.
2. To form the plural, add *-s* to a base word that ends in *x*.
3. Sometimes rhyming words have different spelling patterns.
4. For some words, the singular and plural forms are spelled the same.
5. Adding endings causes some base-word spellings to change.
6. The plural of *bus* is *buses.*
7. To form the plural, add *-es* to a base word that ends in *ch.*
8. Rhyming words have the same ending vowel and consonant sounds.

B. Expanding Your Skill

Read each sentence below. Number your paper from 1 to 5. For each underlined word, write two rhyming words from the box: one that has the same spelling pattern, and one that has a different spelling pattern.

Same Spelling Pattern	Different Spelling Pattern
round	glance
afford	browned
kneading	hair
slants	scored
dare	speeding

1. Gregorian <u>chants</u> are old songs that were first performed by monks.
2. Songs are often learned by listening to the words rather than by <u>reading</u> them.
3. Some types of music are used to accompany <u>square</u> dances.
4. Rock music combines many other types of music into a new <u>sound</u>.
5. A <u>chord</u> is three or more musical notes played simultaneously to create a harmony.

C. Exploring Language

Poetry Read the words to the song below. Then answer the questions that follow.

Oh, say can you see by the dawn's early light
What so proudly we hailed at the twilight's last gleaming?
Whose broad stripes and bright stars thro' the perilous fight,
O'er the ramparts we watched were so gallantly streaming?
And the rocket's red glare, the bombs bursting in air,
Gave proof through the night that our flag was still there.
Oh, say does that star-spangled banner yet wave
O'er the land of the free and the home of the brave?

1. Which rhyming words in the song have the same spelling pattern?
2. Which rhyming words in the song have different spelling patterns?

D. Expressing Yourself

Choose one of these activities. When you are finished, give your paper to your teacher.

1. Write a song about your school. Include rhyming words with the same and different spelling patterns. When you are finished, read your song lyrics aloud to your teacher or your class. Point out the words that rhyme and how each one is spelled.
2. **WORK with a PARTNER** Working with a partner, write the plurals for each word shown in the box below. Then write a nonsense song using all the words. Include rhyming words whenever you can. Sing the song with your partner to your teacher or to your class.

zero	elf	flea	cargo	fox

Unit 3

Visualization Strategy

When some endings are added to base words, the base-word spelling and pronunciation change. Often the spellings do *not* match the way they sound. It is important to know what the correct spelling of the word looks like.

- The /sh/ sound can be spelled *ti, ci,* or *si.*

  infect ⟶ infec**ti**on
  finance ⟶ finan**ci**al
  express ⟶ expres**si**on

- The /əl/ sound can be spelled *-el, -al, -le, -il,* or *-ile.*

  tow**el**, anim**al**, trem**ble**, penc**il**, frag**ile**

Conserve Our Resources

Choose the correct spelling of each word to complete the sentence.

1. _____ is the wise use and protection of Earth's resources.
   (A) Conservasion **(B)** Conservation **(C)** Conservacion

2. The _____ found in the earth are useful resources.
   (A) minerals **(B)** minerils **(C)** minerels

3. As the _____ on Earth grows, the use of our resources increases.
   (A) populacion **(B)** populasion **(C)** population

4. _____ pass laws to prohibit the damage or waste of natural resources.
   (A) Politicians **(B)** Polititians **(C)** Politisians

5. _____, a fuel that powers many trucks, contributes to air pollution.
   (A) Diesil **(B)** Diesal **(C)** Diesel

6. The _____ of the Environmental Protection Agency is to protect the nation's air, water, and land.
   (A) mition **(B)** micion **(C)** mission

Unit 3
Visualization Strategy

Up in the Sky

7. _____ includes the building and flying of aircraft.
(A) Aviacion (B) Aviasion (C) Aviation

8. Planes and helicopters _____ across land and sea to take people and cargo to distant places.
(A) traval (B) travel (C) travil

9. The making of spacecrafts and _____ is a part of the aerospace industry.
(A) missiles (B) missels (C) missils

10. The Wright Brothers made the first piloted aircraft after studying gliders and wind _____.
(A) tunniles (B) tunnels (C) tunnals

11. By the end of the 1930s, airplanes were an important means of _____.
(A) transportacion (B) transportasion (C) transportation

12. Today, airplanes transport about one and a half billion people on an _____ basis.
(A) annuel (B) annuil (C) annual

13. Air travel allows people to be more _____ than ever before.
(A) mobile (B) mobal (C) mobel

14. Flying is an _____ way to get from New York to California.
(A) effisient (B) effitient (C) efficient

15. Airline travel is a _____ means of transport in the modern world.
(A) vital (B) vitile (C) vitel

The Elements

Choose the correct spelling of each word to complete the sentence.

16. _____ gases are found in Earth's atmosphere and occur naturally.
(A) Nobal **(B)** Nobil **(C)** Noble

17. This type of gas can be one of six _____ elements.
(A) chemical **(B)** chemicel **(C)** chemicle

18. There are twenty synthetic, or _____, elements.
(A) artificial **(B)** artifisial **(C)** artifitial

19. One hundred and nine of the one hundred and ten elements have _____ names.
(A) offisial **(B)** official **(C)** offitial

20. Water is made of a _____ of the elements hydrogen and oxygen.
(A) combinasion **(B)** combinacion **(C)** combination

21. _____ people first discovered many elements, like gold and copper.
(A) Antient **(B)** Ansient **(C)** Ancient

22. Some compounds are very _____ and exist only in laboratories.
(A) unstable **(B)** unstabile **(C)** unstabel

23. Most elements are classified as _____.
(A) metals **(B)** metels **(C)** metils

Unit 3
Visualization Strategy

The Tourist

24. A tourist is a person who visits a _____ for pleasure.
(A) destination (B) destinacion (C) destinasion

25. A tourist may visit a monument or have a _____ at the beach.
(A) vacasion (B) vacation (C) vacacion

26. An _____ tourist travels to different countries.
(A) internationel (B) international (C) internationil

27. Some tourists visit special museums to see the _____ of famous people.
(A) possestions (B) possescions (C) possessions

28. _____ jet planes help tourists get from one place to another faster.
(A) Commertial (B) Commersial (C) Commercial

29. Some tourists visit _____ with interesting wildlife and natural beauty.
(A) locations (B) locasions (C) locacions

30. Some tourists risk great _____ to go on adventurous trips.
(A) perel (B) perile (C) peril

31. These tourists may choose adventures on _____ islands.
(A) tropicle (B) tropical (C) tropicel

Unit 3

Visualization Strategy

Sometimes the /zhər/ sound and the /chər/ sound have similar spellings. Think about how words with these sounds look before you spell them.

- The /zhər/ sound at the end of a word can be spelled *-sure.*
  plea**sure**
- The /chər/ sound at the end of a word can be spelled *-ture.*
  pas**ture**

Choose the correct spelling of each word to complete the sentence.

32. Rulers and metersticks are used to _____ length.
    (A) meazhur **(B)** measure **(C)** measher

33. A female tiger _____ her cubs for about two years.
    (A) nursures **(B)** nurchers **(C)** nurtures

34. The height of a _____ poodle ranges from ten to fifteen inches.
    (A) miniature **(B)** miniasure **(C)** miniachur

35. Because a lot of silver and gold were found in Montana's mountains, it is called the _____ State.
    (A) Treachur **(B)** Treazure **(C)** Treasure

36. Abraham Lincoln was a man of great _____.
    (A) statcher **(B)** stature **(C)** stachure

37. Many people play golf in their _____ time.
    (A) leisure **(B)** leishure **(C)** leizure

38. Works of science fiction typically describe events in the _____.
    (A) futcher **(B)** fuchur **(C)** future

39. Historical _____ describes events in the past.
    (A) literachur **(B)** literatchure **(C)** literature

Unit 3
Visualization Strategy

40. Too much ____ to the sun can cause skin damage.
(A) expozure **(B)** exposure **(C)** expochure

41. An ____ is an instrumental piece of music that introduces a longer piece of music.
(A) overture **(B)** overchur **(C)** oversure

42. Many people read books of fiction as a ____ from reality.
(A) deparchur **(B)** deparsure **(C)** departure

43. A cast is often worn to help a bone ____ heal.
(A) fracsure **(B)** fracture **(C)** frachure

44. Celebrations are often held under large, tent-like ____.
(A) enclosures **(B)** enclozures **(C)** enclochurs

45. ____ that appears on blades of grass in the early morning is called dew.
(A) Moisure **(B)** Moisture **(C)** Moischure

46. ____ of all the facts in a case is expected in a court of law.
(A) Discloture **(B)** Disclosure **(C)** Disclozhure

47. The Sears Tower is the tallest ____ in the United States.
(A) structcher **(B)** structshure **(C)** structure

48. Building inspections ____ the safety of workers in a building.
(A) ensure **(B)** enshure **(C)** ensher

Unit 4
Visualization Strategy

Commonly Misspelled Words

Some words you see all the time. The more you see a word, the easier it is to remember how to spell it. Think about how the word looks. If a word does not "look" correct, think of the proper way to spell it.

Hurricanes

Is each underlined word spelled correctly?

1. When a hurricane hits land, it can be quite a catastrofy.
   (A) Yes **(B)** No, change to *catastrophe*

2. Meteorologists are scientists who study the wether.
   (A) Yes **(B)** No, change to *weather*

3. They analyze how a hurricane forms and moves across the ocean.
   (A) Yes **(B)** No, change to *analise*

4. They can tell people if it is nesessary for them to evacuate.
   (A) Yes **(B)** No, change to *necessary*

5. Many people volunteer their time and money to offer relief to hurricane victims.
   (A) Yes **(B)** No, change to *releaf*

6. The efekts of a hurricane can last many months.
   (A) Yes **(B)** No, change to *effects*

7. Hurricanes occur during months when water temperature is warm.
   (A) Yes **(B)** No, change to *temprature*

8. We continue to increase our knowledge of hurricanes every year.
   (A) Yes **(B)** No, change to *knowlege*

9. Scientists continue to do reserch about hurricane behavior.
   (A) Yes **(B)** No, change to *research*

10. A hurricane is an example of an extreme tropical storm.
    (A) Yes **(B)** No, change to *extreem*

Unit 4
Visualization Strategy

Rural Life in India

11. Many people in India live in small villeges.
(A) Yes **(B)** No, change to *villages*

12. The accommodations include brick and mud houses.
(A) Yes **(B)** No, change to *acommodations*

13. On warm nights, naybores sleep outside.
(A) Yes **(B)** No, change to *neighbors*

14. An Indian family posseses fewer things than most American families.
(A) Yes **(B)** No, change to *possesses*

15. Because of the hot climate, people wear light, lose clothing.
(A) Yes **(B)** No, change to *loose*

16. Most villages have their own government.
(A) Yes **(B)** No, change to *goverment*

17. There is one person that the village recognizes as the head of the council.
(A) Yes **(B)** No, change to *recognises*

18. Villages celebrate many diferent holidays throughout the year.
(A) Yes **(B)** No, change to *different*

19. Geography may determine the way the houses look in a village.
(A) Yes **(B)** No, change to *Geografy*

20. Villages may have narrow streets or straight, paralell streets.
(A) Yes **(B)** No, change to *parallel*

21. Schools are built at village borders to provide ampel open spaces.
(A) Yes **(B)** No, change to *ample*

Unit 4

Visualization Strategy

Right to Vote

Is each underlined word spelled correctly?

22. In the United States you are eligibal to vote at eighteen.
(A) Yes **(B)** No, change to *eligible*

23. Voting is a privilidge and a right in the United States.
(A) Yes **(B)** No, change to *privilege*

24. Untill 1920, most women were not allowed to vote.
(A) Yes **(B)** No, change to *Until*

25. A person running for a political office does not have to receive a unanimous vote to win.
(A) Yes **(B)** No, change to *recieve*

26. In most elections, the person who loses concedes to the winner.
(A) Yes **(B)** No, change to *conceeds*

27. Unfortunately, it is unuzual for more than sixty percent of people to vote in an election.
(A) Yes **(B)** No, change to *unusual*

28. Americans in foreign countries can vote by absentee ballot.
(A) Yes **(B)** No, change to *forein*

29. Choosing a candidate to vote for is an important decision.
(A) Yes **(B)** No, change to *decicion*

30. A voter has a voter regestration card to show when voting.
(A) Yes **(B)** No, change to *registration*

31. Many people do not appreciate the importance of the right to vote.
(A) Yes **(B)** No, change to *apreciate*

32. Some foreign countries do not hold free elections.
(A) Yes **(B)** No, change to *ellections*

Unit 4
Visualization Strategy

Choose the correct spelling of each word to complete the sentence.

33. Dentists do not _____ eating sweets.
(A) recommend (B) reccommend (C) recomend

34. People eat at _____ more than ever before.
(A) restarants (B) restauraunts (C) restaurants

35. It is not _____ to throw trash on the ground.
(A) permissable (B) permissible (C) permisibel

36. Farmers _____ like owls because the owls eat rodents that damage crops.
(A) especally (B) espesially (C) especially

37. An _____ is an overstatement of something.
(A) exageration (B) exagerration (C) exaggeration

38. The _____ of Christopher Columbus began in August of 1492.
(A) voyage (B) voyege (C) voyedge

39. The earliest Roman _____ had ten months.
(A) calender (B) calander (C) calendar

40. Harry Potter is a well-known _____.
(A) character (B) charecter (C) charactar

41. A business is often formed as a partnership or a _____.
(A) corperation (B) corporation (C) corparation

42. A _____ or other small business may be owned by one person.
(A) delicatessen (B) dellicatesen (C) delicatesen

Unit 4
Visualization Strategy

Recycling

Choose the correct spelling of each word to complete the sentence.

43. _____ is a material that can be formed into many shapes and can be recycled.
(A) Aluminum **(B)** Alumimum **(C)** Aluminumm

44. Newspaper is another item that _____ can be recycled.
(A) definetly **(B)** definitly **(C)** definitely

45. Many towns _____ recycling days throughout the year.
(A) scedule **(B)** schedul **(C)** schedule

46. The more people who participate in recycling programs, the more _____ the programs will be.
(A) sucsessful **(B)** successful **(C)** sucessful

47. Some people recycle trash into art by creating unique _____.
(A) suprises **(B)** surprizes **(C)** surprises

48. Every year, _____ of pounds of trash are recycled.
(A) millions **(B)** milions **(C)** milliens

49. Recycling materials will _____ Earth's natural resources.
(A) connserv **(B)** conserve **(C)** consserv

50. Recycling helps prevent _____ of the planet's air and water.
(A) pullution **(B)** pollotion **(C)** pollution

Unit 4
Visualization Strategy

Attorney at Law

51. When two people have an _____, they sometimes settle it in a court of law.
(A) arguement **(B)** argument **(C)** argumente

52. A person is _____ until he or she is proven guilty.
(A) innocente **(B)** inocent **(C)** innocent

53. Sometimes a lawyer has an _____ to help research the case.
(A) assistant **(B)** asisstant **(C)** assistent

54. Each side wants to _____ a fair conclusion.
(A) acheeve **(B)** acheive **(C)** achieve

55. Lawyers must speak to the judge using _____ language.
(A) appopriate **(B)** appropriate **(C)** appropreate

56. The judge listens to both sides and then gives the final _____.
(A) judgmente **(B)** judgment **(C)** judjement

57. The side that is accused of a crime is called the _____.
(A) defense **(B)** defence **(C)** defens

58. Being a lawyer can be a difficult _____.
(A) proffesion **(B)** profession **(C)** professioun

The Second LAP
Language Activity Pages

A. Exercising Your Skill

You have been learning about using the visualization strategy to spell words. Number your paper from 1 to 10, and read the sentences below. Each underlined word is misspelled. Use the visualization strategy to help you rewrite the misspelled words correctly.

1. Robert Cormier writes books of fition.
2. Many authors do a lot of research at the libary.
3. The publishing buziness produces many best-selling books.
4. Many authors like to write about real peeple.
5. Writing a novel is a tremendus task.
6. There are some people who think that writing is tortur.
7. Writers need suficient time to think and to write.
8. Competision is often fierce in the publishing world.
9. Some writers never achieve commertial success.
10. Writing is a challenging and rewarding ocupation.

B. Expanding Your Skill

Read the sentences below. Number your paper from 1 to 6. Choose the correct ending for each incomplete word.

1. The first edi_____ of some books are very valuable.
   (A) -tions **(B)** -sions
2. After your class reads a book, you have a discus_____ about it.
   (A) -tion **(B)** -sion
3. Reading a good book brings plea_____ to many people.
   (A) -ture **(B)** -sure
4. *Island of the Blue Dolphins* is a great adven_____ story.
   (A) -ture **(B)** -sure
5. An anthology is a collec_____ of short stories.
   (A) -tion **(B)** -sion
6. Reading a book can be a highly satisfying lei_____ activity.
   (A) -sure **(B)** -zure

C. Exploring Language

Expository Writing Read the following paragraph. Find fifteen misspelled words in the paragraph, and write the correct spelling for each on a separate sheet of paper.

Nobody can claim the tital "the inventor of television." Many people worked on the invention at every levil of design. Often, discoveries were made through trile and error. A sample, or modile, television was developed around 1926 when a Scottish engineer showed his television to the public. A Russian American engineer invented an electronic camera tube that became the foundasion for today's television sets. The finel touches came many years later. Today, many people receive their television signil through an underground cabel. Modern high-definision television systems provide very sharp pictures with littel interference. These systems can link the funcsions of a television with those of a home computer. Some television sets are made to match the furnicher in a room. Large-screen televisions may meazure up to sixty inches wide. There are many classic movies shown on television today, as well as originel programs. Television provides a vitel connection to the world.

D. Expressing Yourself

Choose one of these activities. When you are finished, give your paper to your teacher.

1. Think of ideas for a story about your favorite sport or hobby. Write a short summary of what your story would be about. Include names of characters and the location of the story. Include as many words that end in *-al, -el, -il, -ile, -le, -sure,* and *-ture* as you can. When you are finished, proofread your work. Don't forget to look for misspellings. Then make any necessary corrections.

2. WORK with a PARTNER Brainstorm three ideas for a title for a book about animals. Include at least one word that ends in *-al, -el, -il, -ile, -le, -sure,* or *-ture* in each title. Look at animal pictures in a dictionary or an encyclopedia to help you think of words to use in your titles. Instead you may come up with three titles of your own as your partner does the same. Then compare one another's titles, and combine any related ideas.

Unit 5
Compound Word Strategy

A **compound word** is two words put together to make one word. The spelling of each word stays the same when the words are combined. Break the compound into its two words to spell each word.

road + block = roadblock   camp + fire = campfire

Choose the compound word that best fits each clue.

1. cold weather
   (A) sandstone **(B)** snowstorm **(C)** earthquake

2. machine that raises heavy objects
   (A) forklift **(B)** typewriter **(C)** windmill

3. idea occurring later
   (A) brainstorm **(B)** troubleshoot **(C)** afterthought

4. used when reading
   (A) bookmark **(B)** bookkeeper **(C)** pocketbook

5. someone who causes problems
   (A) homemaker **(B)** upstart **(C)** troublemaker

6. without socks or shoes
   (A) shoelace **(B)** barefoot **(C)** handshake

7. what a person wears to sleep
   (A) raincoat **(B)** bedspread **(C)** nightclothes

8. way of thinking
   (A) viewpoint **(B)** skyline **(C)** landslide

9. direct and honest
   (A) folklore **(B)** forthright **(C)** spearhead

10. special event or marker in life
   (A) homespun **(B)** input **(C)** milestone

Unit 5
Compound Word Strategy

Choose the compound word that is made by joining two shorter words in each sentence.

11. If I don't drink some water, I may fall asleep.
(A) somebody **(B)** waterfall

12. In some games, you have to guard the ball with your body.
(A) bodyguard **(B)** basketball

13. The best way to drive a car is with both hands on the wheel.
(A) carpool **(B)** driveway

14. I made some phone calls while I was at home.
(A) homemade **(B)** homework

15. Don't fall down in the snow.
(A) falloff **(B)** snowfall

16. She gave the paper back to her teacher.
(A) background **(B)** paperback

17. There aren't any gills in the human body.
(A) anybody **(B)** everybody

18. The sun rose over the field of flowers.
(A) overlook **(B)** sunflowers

19. This tool belongs in the red box.
(A) toolbox **(B)** toolshed

20. Our house was hot when we got back from summer vacation.
(A) outback **(B)** hothouse

21. The trees cast broad shadows over the street.
(A) castaway **(B)** broadcast

22. The main feature of the land in Hawaii is volcanoes.
(A) mainland **(B)** landfill

Unit 6
Meaning Strategy

Homophones are words that sound exactly alike but have different meanings and usually have different spellings.

- To spell a homophone correctly, you must know how the word is being used.

  The **weather** was sunny. (not *whether*)

  Squirrels **bury** acorns in the fall. (not *berry*)

Even though a homophone is spelled correctly, double-check the meaning to make sure you are using the correct one.

The Ocean

Choose the correct homophone to complete each sentence.

1. Most full-_____ sea horses are only six inches long.
   (A) groan **(B)** grown

2. Some _____ are capable of holding their breath for two hours.
   (A) wails **(B)** whales

3. A _____ reef is a colorful underwater environment.
   (A) choral **(B)** coral

4. The reef is like a giant _____ for small fish to swim through.
   (A) maize **(B)** maze

5. In the _____, some people enjoy watching the sunrise over the ocean.
   (A) morning **(B)** mourning

6. The ocean's high _____ usually occurs at the same time every day.
   (A) tied **(B)** tide

7. The mountain ranges on the ocean floor are an amazing _____ for divers.
   (A) site **(B)** sight

8. Huge cliffs rise from the ocean floor and create _____ surfaces.
   (A) sheer **(B)** shear

Unit 6

Meaning Strategy

9. Many people work at a job so that they can _____ money.
(A) earn (B) urn

10. On airplanes you can sit next to the _____ or the window.
(A) aisle (B) isle

11. Many people enjoy eating _____ corn right off the cob.
(A) suite (B) sweet

12. In India, vendors often _____ their goods on the street.
(A) pedal (B) peddle

13. The _____ job of the gallbladder is to store bile.
(A) principal (B) principle

14. Jumbo, one of the largest elephants, _____ in at 14,500 pounds.
(A) wade (B) weighed

15. Drum sets usually come with a pair of _____.
(A) cymbals (B) symbols

16. In the army, _____ is the rank between major and general.
(A) colonel (B) kernel

17. Movie film is wound around a _____ and shown with a projector.
(A) real (B) reel

18. Political candidates may become _____ after giving a lot of speeches.
(A) hoarse (B) horse

19. A candidate's _____ arranges the candidate's daily schedule.
(A) aide (B) aid

20. Roasted _____ and cheese may be added to a vegetable pizza.
(A) leaks (B) leeks

Unit 7
Dictionary Strategy

Sometimes prefixes or suffixes sound almost the same. Pronunciation of the word is *not* enough to help you spell it. Use a dictionary to make sure your spelling is correct.

- The prefixes *en-* and *em-* mean "in," "to cause to become," "to give," or "to cover." *Em-* is used before words that begin with *b, m,* or *p.*

  empress

  endear

Choose the prefix that correctly spells each word. Use a dictionary if needed.

1. The word ____*barrass* means "to make someone feel shy."
   (A) *em-* **(B)** *en-*

2. The word ____*power* means "to give power to."
   (A) *em-* **(B)** *en-*

3. The word ____*velop* means "to wrap or cover."
   (A) *em-* **(B)** *en-*

4. An ____*zyme* is a protein in animals that makes chemical reactions occur.
   (A) *em-* **(B)** *en-*

5. The word ____*brace* means "to hug."
   (A) *em-* **(B)** *en-*

6. The word ____*deavor* means "to try."
   (A) *em-* **(B)** *en-*

7. The word ____*bark* means "to start out."
   (A) *em-* **(B)** *en-*

8. The word ____*code* means "to put into code or cipher."
   (A) *em-* **(B)** *en-*

Unit 7

Dictionary Strategy

The prefixes *il-*, *im-*, *in-*, and *ir-* are negative in meaning. When they are added to words, they mean "not."

- *il-* is used before words that begin with *l* — **il**legal
- *im-* is used before words that begin with *b, m,* or *p* — **im**proper
- *ir-* is used before words that begin with *r* — **ir**regular

Choose the prefix that correctly spells each word. Use a dictionary if needed.

9. The word _____*complete* means "not finished."
(A) *il-* **(B)** *im-* **(C)** *in-* **(D)** *ir-*

10. The word _____*lusion* means "appears to exist but does not exist."
(A) *il-* **(B)** *im-* **(C)** *in-* **(D)** *ir-*

11. The word _____*responsible* means "not trustworthy or reliable."
(A) *il-* **(B)** *im-* **(C)** *in-* **(D)** *ir-*

12. The word _____*modest* means "not modest."
(A) *il-* **(B)** *im-* **(C)** *in-* **(D)** *ir-*

13. The word _____*mature* means "not fully grown."
(A) *il-* **(B)** *im-* **(C)** *in-* **(D)** *ir-*

14. The word _____*active* means "being out of use."
(A) *il-* **(B)** *im-* **(C)** *in-* **(D)** *ir-*

15. The word _____*secure* means "not stable or confident."
(A) *il-* **(B)** *im-* **(C)** *in-* **(D)** *ir-*

16. The word _____*partial* means "not favoring one more than another."
(A) *il-* **(B)** *im-* **(C)** *in-* **(D)** *ir-*

17. The word _____*resistible* means "unstoppable or attractive."
(A) *il-* **(B)** *im-* **(C)** *in-* **(D)** *ir-*

Unit 7
Dictionary Strategy

Choose the prefix that correctly spells each word. Use a dictionary if needed.

18. The word _____*literate* means "not able to read."
(A) *il-* **(B)** *im-* **(C)** *in-* **(D)** *ir-*

19. The word _____*rational* means "not logical or sensible."
(A) *il-* **(B)** *im-* **(C)** *in-* **(D)** *ir-*

20. The word _____*dignant* means "angry at something that is not fair."
(A) *il-* **(B)** *im-* **(C)** *in-* **(D)** *ir-*

21. The word _____*mobile* means "not movable."
(A) *il-* **(B)** *im-* **(C)** *in-* **(D)** *ir-*

22. The word _____*balance* means "lack of balance."
(A) *il-* **(B)** *im-* **(C)** *in-* **(D)** *ir-*

23. The word _____*formal* means "casual."
(A) *il-* **(B)** *im-* **(C)** *in-* **(D)** *ir-*

24. The word _____*relevant* means "unimportant."
(A) *il-* **(B)** *im-* **(C)** *in-* **(D)** *ir-*

25. The word _____*sufficient* means "not enough or unacceptable."
(A) *il-* **(B)** *im-* **(C)** *in-* **(D)** *ir-*

26. The word _____*personal* means "unemotional or objective."
(A) *il-* **(B)** *im-* **(C)** *in-* **(D)** *ir-*

27. The word _____*patient* means "abrupt or restless."
(A) *il-* **(B)** *im-* **(C)** *in-* **(D)** *ir-*

28. The word _____*replaceable* means "not able to be replaced."
(A) *il-* **(B)** *im-* **(C)** *in-* **(D)** *ir-*

Unit 7

Dictionary Strategy

Sometimes it helps to know the meaning of the word you are trying to spell. *Mis-* and *dis-* are both prefixes that generally mean "not."

mis- means "wrongly" or "badly" **mis**spell

dis- means "opposite of" **dis**agree

Choose the prefix that correctly spells each word. Use a dictionary if needed.

29. The word _____*content* means "not happy."
 (A) *mis-* **(B)** *dis-*

30. The word _____*conduct* means "bad behavior."
 (A) *mis-* **(B)** *dis-*

31. The word _____*approve* means "to consider not good."
 (A) *mis-* **(B)** *dis-*

32. The word _____*cord* means "a lack of agreement."
 (A) *mis-* **(B)** *dis-*

33. The word _____*connect* means "to separate."
 (A) *mis-* **(B)** *dis-*

34. The word _____*judge* means "to judge wrongly."
 (A) *mis-* **(B)** *dis-*

35. The word _____*take* means "an error or not right."
 (A) *mis-* **(B)** *dis-*

36. The word _____*integrate* means "to fall apart."
 (A) *mis-* **(B)** *dis-*

37. The word _____*courage* means "to warn or to sadden."
 (A) *mis-* **(B)** *dis-*

38. The word _____*lead* means "to deceive or to misinform."
 (A) *mis-* **(B)** *dis-*

Unit 7
Dictionary Strategy

The suffixes *-ible* and *-able* mean "capable of" or "tending to." They have the same pronunciation. It may be necessary to use a dictionary to check your spellings of words with these suffixes.

Choose the suffix that correctly spells each word. Use a dictionary if needed.

39. The word *respons*_____ means "able to be trusted."
    (A) *-ible* **(B)** *-able*

40. The word *indel*_____ means "impossible to remove or erase."
    (A) *-ible* **(B)** *-able*

41. The word *accept*_____ means "worthy of being accepted."
    (A) *-ible* **(B)** *-able*

42. The word *commend*_____ means "worthy of praise."
    (A) *-ible* **(B)** *-able*

43. The word *vis*_____ means "able to be seen."
    (A) *-ible* **(B)** *-able*

44. The word *poss*_____ means "capable of being or happening."
    (A) *-ible* **(B)** *-able*

45. The word *prob*_____ means "likely to happen or be true."
    (A) *-ible* **(B)** *-able*

46. The word *perish*_____ means "subject to decay."
    (A) *-ible* **(B)** *-able*

47. The word *flex*_____ means "bendable or agreeable."
    (A) *-ible* **(B)** *-able*

48. The word *adjust*_____ means "capable of correction or change."
    (A) *-ible* **(B)** *-able*

Unit 7

Dictionary Strategy

The suffixes *-ant* and *-ent* and the suffixes *-ance* and *-ence* sound alike. Pronunciation is *not* enough to help you spell words with these endings. Again, you may need to consult a dictionary for correct spellings.

Choose the suffix that correctly spells each word. Use a dictionary if needed.

49. The word *toler*_____ means "the willingness to respect each other's opinions."
(A) *-ance* **(B)** *-ence*

50. The word *appar*_____ means "easily seen."
(A) *-ant* **(B)** *-ent*

51. The word *appear*_____ means "the act of coming into sight."
(A) *-ance* **(B)** *-ence*

52. The word *resid*_____ means "a place where one lives."
(A) *-ance* **(B)** *-ence*

53. The word *depend*_____ means "relying on someone else."
(A) *-ant* **(B)** *-ent*

54. The word *assist*_____ means "a person who assists."
(A) *-ant* **(B)** *-ent*

55. The word *promin*_____ means "very easily seen."
(A) *-ant* **(B)** *-ent*

56. The word *perman*_____ means "lasting."
(A) *-ance* **(B)** *-ence*

57. The word *transpar*_____ means "sheer or obvious."
(A) *-ant* **(B)** *-ent*

58. The word *turbul*_____ means "frantic or stormy."
(A) *-ant* **(B)** *-ent*

The Third LAP
Language Activity Pages

A. Exercising Your Skill

You have been learning about using the compound word strategy, the meaning strategy, and the dictionary strategy to spell words correctly. Number your paper from 1 to 8. Read the sentences below. Use the meaning strategy to decide which is the correct word to complete each sentence.

1. An injury to the (heal, heel) would make walking difficult.
2. Everybody has a (navel, naval) on their abdomen.
3. Each (vain, vein) in the body brings blood back to the heart.
4. The human body has over 700 (muscles, mussels).
5. Red blood looks (blew, blue) through the skin because of the way light is absorbed by the skin.
6. The base of the skin's upper layer constantly divides to make new (cells, sells).
7. The (principal, principle) artery, or vessel, of the heart is called the aorta.
8. Different colors of (graze, grays) and whites can be seen in the brain.

B. Expanding Your Skill

Use some prefixes and suffixes from the box to complete the spelling of the words below. Write the completed words on a separate sheet of paper.

im-	*in-*	*il-*	*ir-*	*mis-*
dis-	*-ant*	*-ent*	*-ance*	*-ence*

1. _____*digestion* ("unable to digest food")
2. _____*located* ("to put out of joint")
3. _____*mune* ("protected from disease")
4. *subst*_____("what something is made of")
5. *nutri*_____ ("something needed for life and growth")
6. *resist*_____ ("ability to fight against something, such as a disease")
7. _____*represent* ("to give a false impression of someone or something")
8. *domin*_____ ("primary or most important")

C. Exploring Language

Narrative Writing Read the following paragraph. Number your paper from 1 to 8, and use the words in the box to complete each compound word.

stop	up	fore	ball	shoe	hard	wide	ache

I headed to the **(1)** _____park for the big game. I ran onto the field and took my position as **(2)** short_____. The batter hit the ball toward me. Just as I was about to catch the ball, I tripped over my **(3)** _____lace. I fell hard on the ground. Boy, did I have a **(4)** head_____! After the game, my dad took me to the doctor for a **(5)** check_____. There was no **(6)** _____spread damage. My dad made me **(7)** _____go practice for one whole week. That was a real **(8)** _____ship for me.

D. Expressing Yourself

Choose one of these activities. When you are finished, give your paper to your teacher.

1. **WORK with a PARTNER** Write these words on a piece of paper: *impossible, discolor, misstep, appearance, permanent,* and *inferior.* Working with a partner, write one word in each blank in the paragraph below. Then read the paragraph aloud to make sure that it makes sense. Finally, underline these prefixes and suffixes: *dis-, mis, im-, in-, -ance,* and *-ent.*

   One _____ on a sidewalk can make you trip. If you fall and bruise your skin, the skin may _____. Red blood cells in the tiny blood vessels under your skin actually break. The bruised tissues under your skin turn blue. The effect of a bruise is not _____. Don't feel _____ if you fall and get a bruise. It is almost _____ to avoid a few bruises in life. Watch the _____ of your bruise. You'll see the colors fade in the reverse order of the colors of the rainbow—from blue to green to yellow to healthy pink or red tissues under your skin.

2. Correctly form five compound words using this list of words: *back, light, under, beat, moon, bone, heart, ground, wind,* and *pipe.*

Unit 8

Proofreading Strategy

Check your writing carefully for spelling mistakes.

- Words with the /ə/ sound in unaccented syllables can be spelled in many different ways.

  al**o**ud, ferr**e**t, vis**i**t, bac**o**n, foc**u**s, summ**er**, leg**al**

- Words with the /f/ sound can be spelled *gh* or *ph.*

  rou**gh**, gra**ph**

Read each phrase. Choose the phrase with the underlined word that is *not* spelled correctly.

1. **(A)** hot asphalt
   (B) letters of the alfabet
   (C) family photograph
   (D) foreign affairs

2. **(A)** laugh out loud
   (B) tough love
   (C) elefants in Africa
   (D) half of a sandwich

3. **(A)** organ music
   (B) my pet parrot
   (C) the goldin ticket
   (D) circular saw

4. **(A)** niece and nephew
   (B) semestor of school
   (C) planet Earth
   (D) triumph in victory

5. **(A)** fantom shadows
   (B) sink and faucet
   (C) radio announcer
   (D) distinguished scholar

6. **(A)** a humble abode
   (B) read aloud
   (C) an abrupt exit
   (D) a trip obroad

Unit 8
Proofreading Strategy

7. (A) write a paragraph
(B) phase of life
(C) silk and satin
(D) calender year

8. (A) dolfins and whales
(B) photo finish
(C) triangular shape
(D) outdoor thermometer

9. (A) an easier way
(B) plastic sandel
(C) water trough
(D) bank account

10. (A) brother of mine
(B) phone call
(C) physical fitness
(D) a pair of feasants

11. (A) inventor of things
(B) fallen tree
(C) currint events
(D) autumn leaves

12. (A) irregular size
(B) the pharaoh of Egypt
(C) animated character
(D) proper grammer

13. (A) rotten egg
(B) cotton field
(C) good behavior
(D) geograghy test

Unit 8

Proofreading Strategy

Read each phrase. Choose the phrase with the underlined word that is *not* spelled correctly.

14. **(A)** play the <u>fonograph</u>
    (B) a <u>conifer</u> forest
    (C) a recurring <u>cough</u>
    (D) off the <u>cuff</u>

15. **(A)** <u>graf</u> paper
    (B) a <u>mastermind</u>
    (C) monstrous <u>typhoon</u>
    (D) <u>amphibious</u> animals

16. **(A)** sign an <u>autograph</u>
    (B) news <u>reporter</u>
    (C) once <u>bitten</u>
    (D) ask a <u>farmicist</u>

17. **(A)** <u>number</u> one
    (B) partner and <u>conspirater</u>
    (C) <u>orphaned</u> children
    (D) newspaper <u>editor</u>

18. **(A)** mostly <u>forgotten</u>
    (B) never a <u>quittor</u>
    (C) no <u>solicitors</u> allowed
    (D) sew a <u>button</u>

19. **(A)** wide <u>receiver</u>
    (B) please <u>refrain</u>
    (C) on the <u>exterier</u>
    (D) call the <u>physician</u>

20. **(A)** fruit <u>flavor</u>
    (B) first place <u>trophy</u>
    (C) under the <u>paviliun</u>
    (D) golden <u>gophers</u>

Unit 8
Proofreading Strategy

Which sentence does *not* have a spelling error?

21. **(A)** Geografers study where people, plants, and animals live in relation to Earth's features.
(B) Geographers study where people, plants, and animals live in relation to Earth's features.

22. **(A)** They try to discover why certain relationships exist.
(B) They try to discovar why certain relationships exist.

23. **(A)** They facter in the effect of the climate on these relationships.
(B) They factor in the effect of the climate on these relationships.

24. **(A)** They might study a canyun in order to learn how Earth's surface has changed.
(B) They might study a canyon in order to learn how Earth's surface has changed.

25. **(A)** Some people make maps of neighborhoods, cities, states, or countries.
(B) Some people make maps of neighbirhoods, cities, states, or countries.

26. **(A)** Others travel to the tropics or to polor areas.
(B) Others travel to the tropics or to polar areas.

27. **(A)** Types of maps include political, physical, and ralief maps.
(B) Types of maps include political, physical, and relief maps.

28. **(A)** Some geographers study languages and religions.
(B) Some geographers study languages and religiens.

29. **(A)** Others study human populatian growth.
(B) Others study human population growth.

30. **(A)** Agricultural maps show the crops and other prodicts of a region.
(B) Agricultural maps show the crops and other products of a region.

Unit 8

Proofreading Strategy

Which sentence does *not* have a spelling error?

31. **(A)** The telegragh was the first instrument to send messages by wires and electric currents.
    (B) The telegraph was the first instrument to send messages by wires and electric currents.

---

32. **(A)** Samuel Morse cunstructed the first model in 1835.
    (B) Samuel Morse constructed the first model in 1835.

---

33. **(A)** It was an importent form of communication between the United States and Europe.
    (B) It was an important form of communication between the United States and Europe.

---

34. **(A)** Operators sent signals with a device that interrupted the flow of electric current on a wire.
    (B) Operaters sent signals with a device that interrupted the flow of electric current on a wire.

---

35. **(A)** Mechanical printers were also used to translate the signals into words.
    (B) Mechanical printors were also used to translate the signals into words.

---

36. **(A)** An earlier method did not work well at night or in bad weathor.
    (B) An earlier method did not work well at night or in bad weather.

---

37. **(A)** Samuel Morse's telegraph system lasted more than one hundrid years.
    (B) Samuel Morse's telegraph system lasted more than one hundred years.

---

38. **(A)** Eventually the telephone became the fastest way to communicate over long distances.
    (B) Eventually the telefone became the fastest way to communicate over long distances.

Unit 8

Proofreading Strategy

The Symphony Orchestra

39. **(A)** A symphony is a large orchestra that usuelly plays classical music.
(B) A symphony is a large orchestra that usually plays classical music.

---

40. **(A)** Sometimes a pianist plays with the orchestra as a special guest.
(B) Sometimes a pianist plays with the orchestra as a speciel guest.

---

41. **(A)** Many orchestras include brass instruments such as trumpets.
(B) Many orchestras include brass instruments such as trumpits.

---

42. **(A)** Most orchestras do not include saxofones.
(B) Most orchestras do not include saxophones.

---

43. **(A)** Large orchestras have over 100 musicians, while small ones have only fifteen to forty players.
(B) Large orchestras have over 100 musicians, while small ones have only fifteen to forty playors.

---

44. **(A)** Members of the orchestra often dress in formol gowns and tuxedoes.
(B) Members of the orchestra often dress in formal gowns and tuxedoes.

---

45. **(A)** Many people make a career out of playing in orchestras.
(B) Many people make a coreer out of playing in orchestras.

---

46. **(A)** A symphony program may focus on different styles of music.
(B) A symphony program may focos on different styles of music.

---

47. **(A)** Some concerts may emfasize classical music.
(B) Some concerts may emphasize classical music.

---

48. **(A)** Some musical programs may include mainly populer pieces.
(B) Some musical programs may include mainly popular pieces.

Unit 9

Family Strategy

In a word family, words are related because they contain the same base word. Knowing the base of a word will help you learn how to spell related words.

- A base word can have different prefixes, suffixes, and endings added to form many related words.

  dictate, dictionary, dictator, dictation

- When endings are added to base words, sometimes a vowel sound can change. In most vowel-sound changes, only the sound changes while the letter remains the same.

  major, majority (the *a* in *major* has the /ā/ sound, and the *a* in *majority* has the /ə/ sound)

Choose the word that does *not* belong in the family.

1. **(A)** real **(B)** reality **(C)** ally **(D)** realization
2. **(A)** critical **(B)** critic **(C)** criticize **(D)** ritual
3. **(A)** clay **(B)** exclaim **(C)** claim **(D)** disclaim
4. **(A)** understand **(B)** under **(C)** misunderstand **(D)** understanding
5. **(A)** haphazard **(B)** happy **(C)** unhappy **(D)** happiness
6. **(A)** corrupt **(B)** corruption **(C)** erupt **(D)** corruptible
7. **(A)** evidence **(B)** evident **(C)** every **(D)** evidently
8. **(A)** exercise **(B)** executive **(C)** execute **(D)** execution
9. **(A)** form **(B)** fortune **(C)** transform **(D)** formula
10. **(A)** grandeur **(B)** grand **(C)** grandiose **(D)** gratitude
11. **(A)** creak **(B)** recreation **(C)** creature **(D)** creative
12. **(A)** slippery **(B)** slip **(C)** spill **(D)** slipper

Unit 9
Family Strategy

13.	(A) relent	(B) unrelenting	(C) relentless	(D) lending
14.	(A) correction	(B) direct	(C) incorrect	(D) correctable
15.	(A) fuse	(B) confuse	(C) confusion	(D) confusing
16.	(A) romancing	(B) romantic	(C) mania	(D) romance
17.	(A) approve	(B) prove	(C) disapprove	(D) disapproval
18.	(A) relief	(B) belief	(C) disbelief	(D) believable
19.	(A) competition	(B) compete	(C) competitive	(D) petite
20.	(A) decisive	(B) decision	(C) incision	(D) decide
21.	(A) slept	(B) sleek	(C) sleeper	(D) asleep
22.	(A) worry	(B) worrisome	(C) worried	(D) worst
23.	(A) transport	(B) portable	(C) repeat	(D) report
24.	(A) unusual	(B) unity	(C) unite	(D) unit
25.	(A) school	(B) scholar	(C) scheme	(D) schooling
26.	(A) miner	(B) mine	(C) mineral	(D) mind
27.	(A) circuit	(B) civil	(C) circular	(D) circle
28.	(A) pleasant	(B) plead	(C) plea	(D) pleading
29.	(A) criminal	(B) cringe	(C) crime	(D) criminology
30.	(A) reception	(B) recite	(C) receipt	(D) receive

Unit 9
Family Strategy

Farming

Choose the correct base word for each underlined word.

31. During the early 1800s, plantations prospered in the South.
(A) plant **(B)** transplant **(C)** planter **(D)** plantain

32. Crops that do not have steady rainfall often rely on irrigation to supply water.
(A) irrigated **(B)** irrigate **(C)** gate **(D)** irrigating

33. The quality of the soil affects crop production.
(A) productive **(B)** duct **(C)** product **(D)** produce

34. Farmers now rely on machines and skilled labor to work the crops.
(A) arm **(B)** farmed **(C)** farmable **(D)** farm

35. Engineers developed dams to store water so that it would be available for crops.
(A) envelope **(B)** developing **(C)** develop **(D)** development

36. Farming is one of the most important occupations in the world.
(A) occupant **(B)** occupational **(C)** cup **(D)** occupy

37. Sometimes the consumption of a crop is much less than the amount that is grown.
(A) consume **(B)** presumption **(C)** consumer **(D)** consumable

38. The remaining crop is called a surplus.
(A) maintain **(B)** remain **(C)** remnant **(D)** remainder

39. Historians acknowledge that people have kept farm animals for almost 9,000 years.
(A) known **(B)** knowledge **(C)** know **(D)** ledge

40. Many farm animals are kept in enclosed areas called pens.
(A) clue **(B)** closet **(C)** enclosure **(D)** close

Unit 9
Family Strategy

Get Out and Vote

41. There is a <u>limitation</u> to how many times a person can vote for one election.
(A) limit (B) unlimited (C) lime (D) limiting

42. In the early 1900s, there were also some <u>restrictions</u> on who could vote.
(A) restrict (B) restricting (C) strict (D) restricted

43. It is <u>estimated</u> that less than fifty-five percent of Americans regularly vote.
(A) estimation (B) estimating (C) estimate (D) mate

44. <u>Presidential</u> elections seem to attract the most voters.
(A) president (B) preside (C) reside (D) presiding

45. Some towns have town hall meetings to hold <u>discussions</u> about upcoming elections.
(A) discussing (B) discussed (C) excuse (D) discuss

46. Candidates use television ads and <u>promotions</u> to encourage people to vote.
(A) promoting (B) motion (C) promote (D) promoted

47. There are two main <u>political</u> parties in the United States.
(A) politician (B) politics (C) politicize (D) apolitical

48. There are also many smaller <u>national</u> parties that people belong to.
(A) nation (B) nationality (C) national (D) international

49. Citizens of a nation vote for certain people to <u>represent</u> them.
(A) present (B) send (C) presence (D) resend

50. During election campaigns, politicians enjoy <u>competing</u> for votes.
(A) competition (B) come (C) compete (D) competent

Unit 9
Family Strategy

Which word has a vowel-sound change for the given base word?

51. relate
(A) relation (B) relative (C) unrelated

52. ignite
(A) igniting (B) ignited (C) ignition

53. meter
(A) metric (B) centimeter (C) millimeter

54. wise
(A) wisest (B) wisely (C) wisdom

55. declare
(A) undeclared (B) declaring (C) declaration

56. divide
(A) divider (B) division (C) divisor

57. narrate
(A) narrator (B) narrative (C) narration

58. deep
(A) depth (B) deeply (C) deeper

59. decide
(A) decision (B) decided (C) decides

60. revolt
(A) revolution (B) revolting (C) revolted

Unit 9
Family Strategy

Use the word family strategy to determine each base word, and choose its missing vowel.

61. inv_____tation
(A) i **(B)** e **(C)** u

62. adm_____rable
(A) o **(B)** e **(C)** i

63. telesc_____pic
(A) e **(B)** o **(C)** u

64. gr_____vity
(A) a **(B)** e **(C)** o

65. prescr_____ption
(A) e **(B)** i **(C)** u

66. inf_____mous
(A) a **(B)** o **(C)** u

67. organ_____zation
(A) e **(B)** u **(C)** i

68. consp_____racy
(A) e **(B)** y **(C)** i

69. pr_____mitive
(A) e **(B)** i **(C)** a

70. recogn_____tion
(A) a **(B)** e **(C)** i

71. com_____dian
(A) e **(B)** i **(C)** a

72. deleg_____tion
(A) a **(B)** i **(C)** e

Unit 10

Foreign Language Strategy

Many English words come from **Greek roots.** The roots are based on words from the Greek language. Each root has a specific meaning and usually combines with other word parts. Words with Greek roots are easier to spell and understand when broken into their parts.

cycl means "circle," bi**cycle**

astr means "star," **astr**onomy

bio means "life," **bio**logy

meter means "measure," centi**meter**

poli means "city," **poli**tics

ology means "study of," psych**ology**

phon means "sound," micro**phone**

graph means "writing," auto**graph**

tele means "distance," **tele**scope

gen means "birth," **gen**eration

Which word part goes in the blank to correctly spell the word that makes sense in the sentence?

1. A baro_____ is used to measure pressure in the atmosphere.
   (A) meter **(B)** metter **(C)** miter

2. The study of how the sun, moon, planets, and stars relate to life is called _____ology.
   (A) astrr **(B)** atr **(C)** astr

3. The study of sounds that are used in speaking is called _____etics.
   (A) phun **(B)** phon **(C)** fon

4. A _____scope is a tool that magnifies faraway objects so that they can be seen.
   (A) tele **(B)** tela **(C)** teli

5. Aluminum and glass are examples of re_____able materials—or materials that can be used again.
   (A) cicl **(B)** sycl **(C)** cycl

6. Dia_____ is the distance across a circle.
   (A) meeter **(B)** meder **(C)** meter

7. A _____cy is a plan or set of principles established by a government or a business.
   (A) poly **(B)** poli **(C)** pol

Unit 10
Foreign Language Strategy

Each sentence below includes a word with a Greek root. Which sentence does *not* have a spelling error?

8. **(A)** Astronomy is the study of the universe, including the stars and planets.
   (B) Astranauts travel in space to better understand the planets, sun, and stars.

---

9. **(A)** New York City is a thriving metropolis in the United States.
   (B) Polece officers work hard to maintain order in a city.

---

10. **(A)** The study of how traits are passed down is called ginetics.
    (B) Solar energy means that the sun generates heat or electric power.

---

11. **(A)** Ecology is the study of living things and their communities.
    (B) Because it has only one wheel, a unicicle is difficult to ride.

---

12. **(A)** Photasynthesis occurs when plants use the light from the sun as energy.
    (B) The word *photograph* literally means "light writing."

---

13. **(A)** The fourth movement of a symphiny usually has a triumphant sound.
    (B) Compact disc players produce clearer sounds than a phonograph.

---

14. **(A)** The study of objects made by humans in the past is archeollogy.
    (B) A biome is a large area that is home to particular kinds of plants and animals.

---

15. **(A)** Biographies of famous Americans are often best sellers.
    (B) People send telagrams when they need to get an urgent message to someone who is in a remote area.

---

16. **(A)** Musicoligy is the scientific study of music separate from performance or composition study.
    (B) The scientific study of animals is called zoology.

Unit 10
Foreign Language Strategy

Many English words also come from **Latin roots.**

form means "shape," trans**form**

min means "smaller," **min**imum

ped means "feet," **ped**estrian

aud means "to hear," **aud**ience

jud, jur, jus means "law," **jur**y

scri means "to write," **scri**be

port means "to carry," im**port**

vid, vis means "see," **vid**eo

Which word part goes in the blank to correctly spell the word that makes sense in the sentence?

17. The United States Department of _____tice enforces federal laws.
(A) Jus **(B)** Jes **(C)** Jos

18. You can recognize firefighters and police officers by their uni_____.
(A) formes **(B)** phorms **(C)** forms

19. Many schools have an _____itorium so that students can hear guest speakers and school concerts.
(A) awd **(B)** aud **(C)** odd

20. Police usually write a full de_____ption of what happened at the scene of an accident.
(A) schri **(B)** scri **(C)** skri

21. Many people now carry _____able computers with them wherever they go.
(A) port **(B)** pord **(C)** porte

22. Earth's supply of fossil fuels has di_____ished over the years.
(A) mini **(B)** minn **(C)** min

23. The _____estal, or base, of the Statue of Liberty is eighty-nine feet tall.
(A) ped **(B)** pedd **(C)** pet

24. Some people say that there is no _____tification, or reason, for using atomic weapons.
(A) jes **(B)** jus **(C)** jos

25. Geese fly in _____ation when they migrate south for the winter.
(A) formm **(B)** form **(C)** phorm

Unit 10
Foreign Language Strategy

Each sentence below includes a word with a Latin root. Which sentence does *not* have a spelling error?

26. **(A)** After hearing a presidential speech, the audience usually claps.
(B) Some very high-pitched sounds are only adible to dogs.

---

27. **(A)** The United States exportes wheat to countries around the world.
(B) A television guide usually lists all the programs by date and time.

---

28. **(A)** Proofreading is a good way to check for mynor errors in your writing.
(B) Scientists search for evidence to support their theories.

---

29. **(A)** Legislators often pass new laws to update and rephorm old laws.
(B) Across the United States, doctors write millions of prescriptions.

---

30. **(A)** Miniature horses have become a very popular breed.
(B) It is up to twelve jerors to decide if a person is guilty or innocent of a crime.

---

31. **(A)** Many movies begin with just a written script.
(B) Before children learn how to write letters and numbers, they first learn how to scrubble.

---

32. **(A)** Many large hotels have porters who carry guests' bags to their rooms.
(B) People who wear glasses usually have their vizion tested every year.

---

33. **(A)** Nurses may injire their backs when lifting patients.
(B) Wrongful treatment of someone may be an injury under the law.

---

34. **(A)** In 1994, Vice President Al Gore coined the term the "Infirmation Superhighway."
(B) The Vice President's speech was transported over the World Wide Web.

Unit 10

Foreign Language Strategy

Many English words come from the German and French languages. However, instead of borrowing root words with specific meanings, the English language adopted some of their spelling patterns.

- German words often have the /ûr/ sound spelled *er* and *ur,* the /əl/ sound spelled *el,* and the /ou/ sound spelled *au* or *ow.*

  ham**bur**ger pretz**el** s**au**erkr**au**t ch**ow**der

- French words often have the /ā/ sound spelled *e, ee, et* (*t* is silent), and *ai.*

  caf**é** entr**ée** gourm**et** mayonn**ai**se

Choose the sentence with the underlined word that is spelled correctly.

35. **(A)** Ballee is a type of theatrical dance that is very graceful and elegant.
(B) Ballet is a type of theatrical dance that is very graceful and elegant.

36. **(A)** A semestur usually lasts about sixteen weeks.
(B) A semester usually lasts about sixteen weeks.

37. **(A)** A fiancée is a woman who is engaged to be married.
(B) A fiancai is a woman who is engaged to be married.

38. **(A)** Strudal is a popular pastry in Austria.
(B) Strudel is a popular pastry in Austria.

39. **(A)** When applying for a job, you need to write a résumé which shows your past experience.
(B) When applying for a job, you need to write a résumet which shows your past experience.

40. **(A)** A frankfurter is another name for a hot dog.
(B) A frankferter is another name for a hot dog.

41. **(A)** In 1897, the inventor demonstrated his new diesel engine.
(B) In 1897, the inventor demonstrated his new diesle engine.

Unit 10

Foreign Language Strategy

Many words in the English language have adopted spelling patterns from the Italian and Spanish languages. Many Italian and Spanish words end with a vowel, and many words contain double consonants.

- Italian: pian**o**, pi**zz**a
- Spanish: avocad**o**, bu**rr**o

Choose the sentence with the underlined word that is spelled correctly.

42. **(A)** An oboe is a type of woodwind instrument.
(B) An obow is a type of woodwind instrument.

43. **(A)** Many hikers and campers wear ponches in order to stay dry from rainy weather.
(B) Many hikers and campers wear ponchos in order to stay dry from rainy weather.

44. **(A)** Italian broccoli is the type that is mostly eaten in the United States.
(B) Italian brocoli is the type that is mostly eaten in the United States.

45. **(A)** Many restaurants have patios where people eat outside.
(B) Many restaurants have pattios where people eat outside.

46. **(A)** Many people enjoy eating spagheti with sauce and meatballs.
(B) Many people enjoy eating spaghetti with sauce and meatballs.

47. **(A)** A corall is a small fenced area used to keep cattle.
(B) A corral is a small fenced area used to keep cattle.

48. **(A)** The word *cofeteria* comes from the Spanish for "coffee shop."
(B) The word *cafeteria* comes from the Spanish for "coffee shop."

49. **(A)** A banister is the handrail at the side of a staircase.
(B) A banuster is the handrail at the side of a staircase.

50. **(A)** Ancient Romans used geese as sentinols, or guards.
(B) Ancient Romans used geese as sentinels, or guards.

The Last LAP

Language Activity Pages

A. Exercising Your Skill

You have been learning about using the proofreading strategy, the family strategy, and the foreign language strategy to spell words. Number your paper from 1 to 10. Use the proofreading strategy to find the misspelled word in each sentence below, and then rewrite it correctly.

1. The pitza originated in Naples, Italy.
2. The people of Mexico enjoy flat breads called torteeyas.
3. The people of France enjoy eating a crescent-shaped roll called a croysant.
4. The Italian word for *dough* is posta.
5. To prevent cabbage from spoiling, Germans soaked it in vinegar to create sourkrout.
6. The word *macoroni* comes from the Italian word for "dumpling."
7. Many people like to dip chips in a spicy Spanish sauce called *salse.*
8. Chocolate mouse is a popular French dessert.
9. *Zuchini* is an Italian word for a dark green summer squash.
10. Good chilli can be made with peppers and vegetables or meat.

B. Expanding Your Skill

Number your paper from 1 to 10. Write the base word of each of the following words.

1. creation
2. preservation
3. traditional
4. appetizer
5. specialties
6. tendency
7. shipment
8. hearty
9. inclined
10. festivity

C. Exploring Language

Personal Writing Read the journal entry below. Number your paper from 1 to 12. Use the word parts in the box to correctly spell each incomplete word.

en	on	er	or
al	le	gh	ph

The class trip to the zoo today was a lot of fun. My **(1)** fav_____ite **(2)** anim_____ is the elephant. I got to touch one of them! Its skin felt very **(3)** rou_____. I learned that there are two **(4)** differ_____t kinds of elephants. Our teacher gave us a short **(5)** geogra_____y lesson to explain where African and Asian elephants live. African elephants are a **(6)** litt_____ bigger than Asian elephants. Their ears are much **(7)** larg_____. Both kinds of elephants are big and **(8)** tou_____! The elephant is the largest **(9)** mamm_____ that lives on land in the world. There used to be over one **(10)** milli_____ elephants in Africa, but today there are only about half that number. We watched one African elephant use his long trunk to take a **(11)** show_____. He squirted water all over himself. Back at school, we had a class **(12)** discussi_____ to talk about our trip.

D. Expressing Yourself

Choose one of these activities. When you are finished, give your paper to your teacher.

1. Write the following base words in a row across the top of your paper: *belief, real, understand,* and *happy.* Think of as many words as you can that belong to each word family. Write the words in columns under the appropriate base word.

2. **WORK with a PARTNER** Find a newspaper and a magazine. Working with a partner, write down on a separate sheet of paper all the words you see that have Greek and Latin roots, or French, German, Italian, or Spanish spelling patterns. Keep a tally of the words to see which language is used most frequently.

SPELLING Scope and Sequence • *Specific Skill Series for Language Arts*

Unit/Level	Level A	Level B	Level C	Level D	Level E	Level F	Level G	Level H
Unit 1	Pronunciation Strategy	Pronunciation Strategy	Pronunciation Strategy	Rhyming Strategy	Rhyming Strategy	Conventions Strategy	Conventions Strategy	Conventions Strategy
Unit 2	Pronunciation Strategy	Pronunciation Strategy	Pronunciation Strategy	Conventions Strategy	Conventions Strategy	Visualization Strategy	Visualization Strategy	Visualization Strategy
Unit 3	Pronunciation Strategy	Pronunciation Strategy	Pronunciation Strategy	Conventions Strategy	Visualization Strategy	Visualization Strategy	Visualization Strategy	Visualization Strategy
Unit 4	Visualization Strategy	Pronunciation Strategy	Rhyming Strategy	Visualization Strategy	Visualization Strategy	Meaning Strategy	Meaning Strategy	Meaning Strategy
Unit 5	Visualization Strategy	Vowel Substitution Strategy	Rhyming Strategy	Visualization Strategy	Compound Word Strategy	Dictionary Strategy	Dictionary Strategy	Dictionary Strategy
Unit 6	Visualization Strategy	Vowel Substitution Strategy	Conventions Strategy	Visualization Strategy	Meaning Strategy	Proofreading Strategy	Proofreading Strategy	Proofreading Strategy
Unit 7	Consonant Substitution Strategy	Consonant Substitution Strategy	Conventions Strategy	Compound Word Strategy	Dictionary Strategy	Family Strategy	Family Strategy	Family Strategy
Unit 8	Vowel Substitution Strategy	Rhyming Strategy	Visualization Strategy	Meaning Strategy	Proofreading Strategy	Foreign Language Strategy	Foreign Language Strategy	Foreign Language Strategy
Unit 9	Rhyming Strategy	Rhyming Strategy	Visualization Strategy	Dictionary Strategy	Family Strategy			
Unit 10	Rhyming Strategy	Conventions Strategy	Visualization Strategy	Proofreading Strategy	Foreign Language Strategy			
Unit 11	Conventions Strategy	Conventions Strategy	Compound Word Strategy	Family Strategy				
Unit 12	Conventions Strategy	Conventions Strategy	Meaning Strategy	Foreign Language Strategy				
Unit 13		Compound Word Strategy	Dictionary Strategy					
Unit 14		Meaning Strategy	Family Strategy					
Unit 15			Family Strategy					